AMERICA'S MOST WINNING TEAMS
NOTRE DAME FOOTBALL

DANIEL E. HARMON

rosen publishing's
rosen central®

New York

Published in 2014 by The Rosen Publishing Group, Inc.
29 East 21st Street, New York, NY 10010

Copyright © 2014 by The Rosen Publishing Group, Inc.

First Edition

Library of Congress Cataloging-in-Publication Data

Harmon, Daniel E.
Notre Dame football/author Daniel E. Harmon.—First edition.
   pages cm.—(America's most winning teams)
Includes bibliographical references and index.
ISBN 978-1-4488-9399-7 (library binding)—ISBN 978-1-4488-9436-9 (pbk.)—
ISBN 978-1-4488-9437-6 (6-pack)
1. University of Notre Dame—Football—History—Juvenile literature. 2. Notre Dame Fighting Irish (Football team)—History—Juvenile literature. I. Title.
GV958.U54H37 2014
796.332'630977289—dc23

2012047203

Manufactured in the United States of America

CPSIA Compliance Information: Batch #S13YA: For further information, contact Rosen Publishing, New York, New York, at 1-800-237-9932.

CONTENTS

INTRODUCTION

Two fierce college football rivals faced off on the gridiron the first Saturday in September 2012 for their season opener. On that cool, festive afternoon, the Notre Dame Fighting Irish beat the Midshipmen of the United States Naval Academy. Notre Dame and Navy have competed in football each year since 1914.

Notre Dame fans are always thrilled by a victory over Navy—usually the underdog, but a pesky one that sometimes scores stunning upsets. This victory was special for Fighting Irish followers. The game was played in Dublin, Ireland.

Interestingly, the university's origins are French, not Irish. The Irish connection did not become firmly fixed at Notre Dame until eighty years after the school's founding. French Catholic missionaries led by the Reverend Edward Sorin established a school in the Indiana wilderness in 1842 and named it L'Université de Notre Dame du Lac ("The University of Our Lady of the Lake"). From then until now, only some of the faculty, coaches, and students have come from either Irish or Catholic backgrounds. Students of other nationalities and faiths are welcomed.

In its early decades, the school offered grade-level and trade labor training. Advanced programs in classical studies (languages, history, law, philosophy, sciences, etc.) were not

Theo Riddick carries the ball for the Fighting Irish in their 2012 victory over Navy. The game, played in Ireland, was the first victory of Notre Dame's undefeated regular season.

very important on the American frontier. Gradually, the number of classical courses increased.

As for its football program, it started with approximately nothing. During its first seven years, beginning in 1887, the Notre Dame team did not even have a coach. From 1890 to 1892, it fielded no team at all. But when Notre Dame did begin serious college play, it quickly established a winning tradition.

During the 1920s, enthusiastic Notre Dame fans began calling their sports teams the "Fighting Irish." A Notre Dame graduate, Francis Wallace, who wrote sports columns for the *New York Daily News*, made the term popular in college football talk. The leprechaun—the elflike symbol of Irish folklore—became the school's sports mascot in the 1960s. Notre Dame's sports logo shows a little man dressed in a green suit and shamrock cap, fists raised, eager to do battle.

Notre Dame University today is the home of some twelve thousand students of diverse backgrounds. Football is just one of twenty-six varsity sports at Notre Dame, and its athletics program is only one part of Notre Dame's famous heritage. The university consistently ranks high among U.S. universities in academic surveys.

To many outsiders, though, any mention of Notre Dame brings to mind Fighting Irish football. More players from Notre Dame have won the coveted Heisman Trophy than from any other university. From Coach Knute Rockne and the Gipper to latter-day all-American inspirations, the Notre Dame football program has been the subject of countless articles, books, and films. Notre Dame is truly legendary among America's most winning football teams.

CHAPTER 1

NOTRE DAME TAKES THE FIELD

The origins of American football are vague. Many of its roots are in the historic English sport of rugby. American Indians, too, influenced it with their hard-nosed field play in "lacrosse," as French settlers termed it.

When Rutgers and Princeton played the first inter-collegiate football game in 1869, the sport was very different from what it is today. It was more like soccer. Players could kick the ball or bat it with their hands, but they were not allowed to run with it. There were no offenses, defenses, or "plays." The game was played nonstop. Each team had twenty-five men on the field. They wore no uniforms. Rutgers players wore red shirts or caps to identify themselves.

One of the few similarities was the construction of goalposts: two uprights connected by a crossbar at each end of the field. But the goalposts functioned much like soccer nets. The objective was to kick the ball under the bar. A successful kick earned one point.

Rutgers won the historic contest, 6–4. In a rematch the next week, Princeton won, 8–0.

Unpadded players, brute force, and confusing melees characterized football in the 1800s. In this Thanksgiving Day game in 1879 between Yale and Princeton, teammates easily recognized one another by wearing the same colors.

WARFARE WITHOUT WEAPONS

In the early years, coaches were merely consultants. The real decision makers were the captains, elected by their teammates. Team captains decided which athletes would play. At many schools, they could fire their coaches.

Over the next twenty-five years, teams gradually agreed on a system of rules that resulted in modern football. The recognized rule-making leader was Walter Camp, a player at Yale.

By the 1890s, each team fielded eleven players at a time. They faced off along a scrimmage line (refined from the "scrum" concept in rugby). A quarterback called signals, and the center kicked the ball back to him to begin each play. The

FOOTBALL IN THE 1880S

College football fans today are accustomed to game day tailgating, stirring band music, and a lovely green, fragrant, precisely chalked field. Members of every team are expected to train year-round to achieve "Mr. Universe" figures. They compete in fashionable, moisture-wicking jerseys and scientifically engineered padding. Professional officials enforce a complex system of rules. Spectators and analysts review and study every play in televised slow motion from three or four angles.

When Notre Dame played its first game against the University of Michigan in 1887, college football was nothing like that. Perhaps a few hundred fans stood around the field; there were no bleachers. Players wore no pads or even helmets. Football fields were marred by rocks and holes; the grass on many college gridirons was patchy. There might (or might not) be a referee or two.

Play was savage, but the players understood it was only a game. Many opposing athletes became lifelong friends. Win or lose, they often got together after the game—some of them with bloodied noses, blackened eyes, and fractured bones—for a rousing dinner and songfest.

quarterback struggled fiercely to advance the ball, with his teammates pulling him forward and opponents pushing him back. The offense had to move the ball five yards in three downs; if they failed, the other team took over.

Players who started a game were expected to finish it. They played both offense and defense. A substitution was made only if a player became disabled.

Even with rules, early football was unruly. Many plays ended in bare-knuckle brawls. Officials were not regularly on hand until 1887. Few penalties were enforced. Roughing the passer, for example, was not considered a rule violation until 1914.

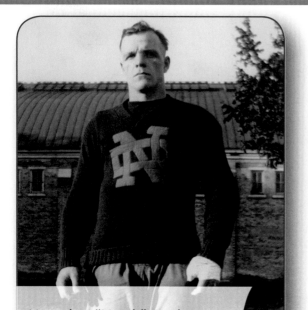

Heartley "Hunk" Anderson played guard at Notre Dame (1918–1921) and in the pros before becoming a coach. His head coaching record at his alma mater (1931–1933) was 16-9-2.

At some schools, coaches taught their athletes to play rough. James McWeeney, the Notre Dame head coach in 1899, told his running backs to grip the ball tightly under one arm and keep the other fist clinched. Some rivalries turned so violent that school administrations banned the contests.

There were no helmets and no effective pads. Players found that they could reduce head shocks simply by growing their hair long. Trousers of thick moleskin made leg bruises less painful.

Broken bones were common. Players frequently were crippled. Some died. In 1905, nineteen players were killed playing American football. (At that time, there were only a fraction as many players as there are now.) As a result, President Theodore Roosevelt demanded more sophisticated rules to make the game safer.

NOTRE DAME JOINS THE FRAY

By 1887, Notre Dame had the makings of a varsity football team, but it was woefully inexperienced. A University of Michigan squad rode to South Bend that year to give Notre Dame its first try in intercollegiate competition. The result was predictable: an 8–0 victory for the Wolverines. Notre Dame played no other games that year.

For the next seven years, it played few games and made little progress as a football contender. After recruiting its first coach in 1894, it began to win occasionally—but some of its opponents were high school teams.

Notre Dame took its first notable strides in intercollegiate football when a twenty-two-year-old student-instructor arrived on campus in 1896 to study law and teach in the English department. Frank Hering was an experienced semi-professional quarterback who had coached for a year at Bucknell University. As a player-coach, he guided Notre Dame to a 12-6-1 record in three seasons. Hering also coached baseball and started the university's basketball program in the winter of 1897–98.

Although his time at Notre Dame was short and his record unspectacular, Hering is remembered as the Father of Notre Dame Football. Hering persuaded university administrators to verify players' student standings. Until then, many college football players weren't students at all, but "tramp" athletes who played for bets and for seats at victory banquet tables. Hering also insisted on presentable uniforms, good equipment, and a playing field purged of rocks.

THE FIRST DECADES

After Hering left, Notre Dame had a dozen head football coaches—a new one every two years, on average. Still, its ragtag football program was beginning to mature. It went undefeated in 1909.

A major turning point occurred in 1913, when the juggernaut Army team invited no-name Notre Dame to fill out its schedule with a game in West Point, New York. Knute Rockne, Notre Dame's left end, and quarterback Gus Dorais, his roommate, had been perfecting the forward pass as an

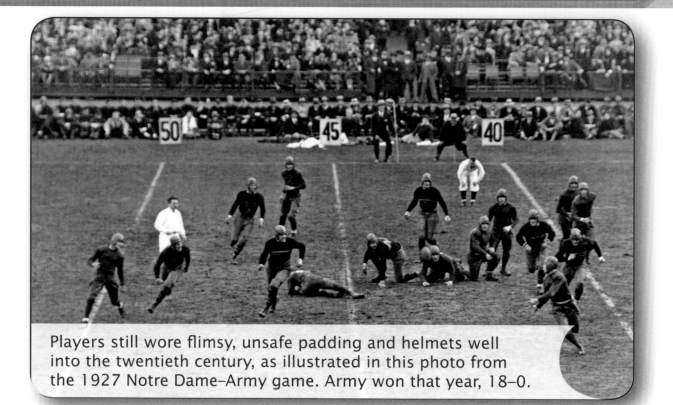

Players still wore flimsy, unsafe padding and helmets well into the twentieth century, as illustrated in this photo from the 1927 Notre Dame–Army game. Army won that year, 18–0.

offensive weapon. During the summer of 1913, they had gotten jobs at a Lake Erie vacation resort. In their free time, they went onto the beach and practiced throwing and catching the ball. Dorais developed his accuracy as the passer, while Rockne became a confident, sure receiver. Returning to campus, they trained a running back to be a backup receiver.

Their great demonstration came against Army. Odds-makers were sure Army would defeat Notre Dame easily—but they did not count on the new passing game. Tossing the ball alternately to his two receivers, Dorais thoroughly confused the Army defense. Notre Dame won, 35–13.

Knute Rockne earned fame as a player at Notre Dame. He would earn far greater stature in football history beginning six years later, when he took over as head coach.

CHAPTER 2

BIRTH OF A COLLEGE FOOTBALL POWERHOUSE

Sports historians point to the stunning upset of Army in 1913 as the beginning of Notre Dame's rise to gridiron greatness. The victory also signaled an important change in the way college football was played. Before, the strongest team almost always won by running the ball, mercilessly beating down weaker opponents. Dorais and Rockne proved that with an effective passing attack, a lightweight squad could become a powerhouse of a different sort.

KNUTE ROCKNE: A STUDENT OF MANY TALENTS

Rockne was twenty-two years old when he was admitted to Notre Dame in September 1910. It did not bother him that Notre Dame was considered a Catholic institution and his family members were Lutherans. Adapting to campus life, though, was difficult. Rockne was bashful by nature. He felt especially embarrassed that he was four years older than most other students in his class.

HARD WORK BRINGS SUCCESS

Lars Rockne was a cart maker who immigrated to America from Norway in 1891 and found work in Chicago. Two years later, his wife, Martha, and their three children joined him. Their son Knute was five years old.

Knute was an outstanding student, despite knowing little English. He was also a willing worker. As a child, he got jobs washing school windows, picking farm vegetables, and delivering purchases for a Chicago department store.

He eagerly took to sports. In high school, he fared poorly at football but better at track. At the end of his junior year, he dropped out of school to take a good-paying job at the central post office in Chicago. He worked night shifts so that he could participate in track with two city athletic clubs.

Growing into manhood, Rockne became an avid reader. He realized the need to further his education and boldly applied for admission to Notre Dame. Because he had not finished high school, he had to take a special entrance examination. To his great joy, he passed.

But he was also apprehensive. Rockne arrived on campus friendless and uncertain about what lay ahead—yet determined to succeed.

His family, working-class immigrants from Norway, could do little to support him in college. He got jobs as a janitor and science lab assistant to pay for his education. He also boxed in barroom prizefights, sometimes earning $20—handsome pay at the time—when he won. Rockne was thrifty with his money. On his occasional excursions from the campus into South Bend, he would walk the 2 miles (3.2 kilometers) rather than pay five cents to ride a trolley.

Rockne ("Rock," to his teammates) was only 5 feet 8 inches (1.7 meters) tall and weighed a boyish 160 pounds (72.6 kilograms) when he tried out for varsity football his sophomore year. In time, with his grit and keen understanding of the sport, he became an exceptional left end. He rose to national attention as a player, making third team all-American in 1913.

In addition to football, he was a pole-vaulting record setter on the Notre Dame track team. Rockne was a man of many talents besides athletics. He starred in student plays, wrote for the school newspaper, and played the flute. Meanwhile, he excelled in class.

Coach Knute Rockne demonstrates blocking tactics to his players personally, wearing no helmet or pads. This photo was taken during a 1925 practice.

After graduating magna cum laude (with great distinction) in 1914, he became a chemistry instructor at Notre Dame. He also helped coach football and track. In 1918, Rockne became head football coach.

ROCKNE MOLDS A NATIONAL FOOTBALL CHAMPION

Knute Rockne introduced several strange but effective ideas to football. One was to start a game with second-string players. Their job was to keep the score as close as possible while tiring out the opposing starters. When Notre Dame's first team took the field later in the game, they had a tremendous physical advantage.

Another Rockne innovation was shifting his offensive backfield, having his backs quickly change positions in the few seconds between lining up and snapping the ball. Rockne perfected the tactic of brush blocking—lightly blocking a defensive lineman, then pushing ahead to run interference downfield for the running back. He had his players wear silk jerseys, making it more difficult for opponents to grab them.

Such refinements, however, were not the main things that made Notre Dame a college football power. Hard work was the key, and Rockne led by example. As a coach in his thirties—an "old man," by football standards—Rockne, wearing no pads, demonstrated full-contact tackling and blocking to his players at practice.

During Rockne's years as head coach, from 1918 to 1930, Notre Dame had a .881 winning percentage with a record of 105-12-5. It remains the best career record for a coach in either college or professional football. Under Rockne, Notre Dame went undefeated five years and won the national championship three times. He coached fifteen all-American players.

Besides coaching football, he served as Notre Dame's athletics director, track coach, trainer, and director of intramural athletics. He even managed the athletics department's business matters, including ticket sales. Meanwhile, he taught chemistry courses and helped run the chemistry lab. Rockne did not have a personal secretary. He answered the sports department telephone and wrote his own letters by hand.

Notre Dame paid Rockne $12,000 per year—a good but not extravagant salary at the time. As a husband and the father of four children, he had to earn extra money during the off-season. Among other work, he wrote a newspaper column and gave speeches.

SHORT ON SUPPLIES

Colleges in times past had little money to budget for their athletics programs. Coach Rockne recalled a game in which a lineman was hurt. The team had only one roll of medical tape, and the injury required the entire roll. Shortly afterward, another player was injured. To bandage his wound, teammates had to remove some of the tape from the first player.

"As coach and athletic director," he later wrote, "I determined that Notre Dame football players would have the best we could afford."

A COACHING LEGEND CUT SHORT

Rockne was confident that Notre Dame was on the brink of national fame as a football power. Despite the stock market crash in 1929, he persuaded university leaders to invest in the construction of Notre Dame Stadium, designed to seat sixty thousand fans. (Expanded in 1997, the tan brick landmark seats more than eighty thousand today.) Until then, the few hundred fans attending a game stood encircling the field. When Rockne died two

The Fighting Irish marching band performs during pregame activities at the modern-day Notre Dame Stadium. The facility is a noted landmark among college football programs.

years later, the Fighting Irish were playing before massive crowds, sometimes at professional sports stadiums. Rockne's impact on the athletics program has lasted into the twenty-first century.

He was only forty-three when he was killed in an airplane crash on March 31, 1931. Tens of thousands of people stood outside Sacred Heart Church at his funeral in South Bend. The entire nation mourned. Newspaper editorials from coast to coast paid him tribute. Within a year, eight biographies of Rockne were published.

It would be another decade, though, before Notre Dame would return to the top in college football.

CHAPTER 3

LEADERS ON THE SIDELINES

For ten years after Knute Rockne's death, Notre Dame fielded creditable football teams under head coaches Heartley Anderson and Elmer Layden. Neither coach achieved Rockne's success, however.

The administration in 1941 hired a man who would lead Notre Dame back to national prominence—and dominance—on the gridiron. Frank Leahy was the second of Notre Dame's most successful and popular coaches.

FRANK LEAHY

As a player, Leahy became a standout lineman on coach Knute Rockne's last three teams. After graduation, he served eight years as assistant coach at three universities. Then, as head coach at Boston College for two years, he steered that team to twenty victories against only two losses.

Impressed by his success, Notre Dame athletics officials hired him as head football coach in 1941. They believed he could bring new life to their football program—and they were right.

Leahy devoted his life completely to football. He sometimes stayed so late at night in his athletics

Frank Leahy plays the center position during a 1928 practice under the eyes of Coach Knute Rockne. Fifteen years later, Leahy was following in Rockne's footsteps, coaching the Irish to greatness.

department office that he slept on top of his desk. Not surprisingly, he was a strict coach who demanded the very best from his players.

In his first season as coach at his alma mater, Leahy's team won eight games and lost none; the only disappointment was a tie. Their record the next year was 7-2-2. In 1943, Notre Dame lost one game but won the national championship—the first of four championship seasons under his guidance.

Leahy interrupted his career, joining the Navy during World War II. When he returned to Notre Dame in 1946, he resumed his winning ways. In his eleven seasons, his Notre

Dame teams went undefeated six times. His overall head coaching record of 107-13-9 made him the second most winning coach in NCAA Division I football—bested only by the record of Knute Rockne.

Perhaps it was partly Leahy's grueling hours and relentless dedication to the sport that led to his abrupt departure from coaching when he was only forty-five. At halftime in the 1953 game against Georgia Tech, he crumpled in the locker room, stabbed by abdominal pain. Leahy completed the season as head coach, then resigned. He lived twenty years longer and briefly served as general manager of a professional team, but he did not coach again.

ARA PARSEGHIAN

After Leahy resigned, the Notre Dame football program lapsed into ten comparatively average seasons, although it was nationally ranked in 1954 and 1955. The athletics department searched for a coach who could return the university to gridiron glory. At last, they identified their man— standing on the opposing sidelines in an intense rivalry.

Northwestern football teams beat Notre Dame four years in a row from 1960 to 1963. Notre Dame's solution: hire away their coach, Ara Parseghian. Parseghian brought another golden age to Fighting Irish football, leading his teams to a 95-17-4 record, two national championships, and five major bowls in eleven seasons. He coached forty-four all-American players.

Parseghian had been a star halfback at Miami University (Ohio) and played for the Cleveland Browns in the National Football League before suffering a career-ending injury. Soon afterward, he was hired as head coach at his old university, Miami. He coached thirteen seasons there and at Northwestern

Players carry Coach Ara Parseghian from the field after Notre Dame's victory over Texas in the 1971 Cotton Bowl. It was sweet revenge—Texas had beaten the Irish in the 1970 Cotton Bowl.

before accepting the job in South Bend. For the next eleven years, he led the Fighting Irish to new heights.

When Parseghian was hired after the 1963 season, Notre Dame had amassed a dismal record of 14-25 over the previous four years. Its 1963 season had been particularly humiliating: two victories, seven losses. Parseghian knew his work was cut out for him. His objective for his first season at Notre Dame was not very ambitious. He simply wanted to post a winning record for a change. Many fans doubted he could do it.

To their delight, he achieved much more. In 1964, the Fighting Irish not only reversed their win-loss record, they

NOTRE DAME VERSUS NOTRE DAME

A fun tradition for football players and fans at many colleges and universities is the annual Spring Game. The climax of spring training, it pits a team's offense against its defense. (The defense is awarded points for stops and turnovers.)

The outcome of the Spring Game means little to a football program. Spring Games are intended to give coaching staff additional information about the strengths and weaknesses of individual players and game strategies. The games also give anxious supporters something to cheer and talk about in the off-season.

In 2007, honorary coaches at Notre Dame's Spring Game were two of its beloved past leaders: Ara Parseghian and Lou Holtz.

Holtz's squad won.

came within a hair of the national championship. Notre Dame was ranked number one in the country with nine victories, no losses, and no ties going into its last game against the University of Southern California on USC's home field. Its victory string included lopsided shutouts of traditional rivals Michigan State and Navy. Southern Cal, however, eked out a 20–17 upset, spoiling Notre Dame's perfect season.

Parseghian's Irish earned for him that elusive perfect season nine years later, capped by a Sugar Bowl victory over Alabama.

Parseghian resigned because of health problems in 1974. He became a television sports analyst and private businessman.

Notre Dame hired Dan Devine, coach of the professional Green Bay Packers, to replace Parseghian. During his six years at the university, Devine was not one of Notre Dame's most popular football coaches. This is surprising because his teams posted a fine overall record (53-16-1), won three postseason bowls, and added another national championship in 1977.

LOU HOLTZ

Fighting Irish football again slipped into a spell of patchy performances after its triumphs under Parseghian and Devine. Then, in 1986, the university hired another veteran coach with an especially colorful record of success. Lou Holtz would lead Notre Dame to its most recent era of football dominance.

Holtz had been head coach at William & Mary, North Carolina State, Arkansas, and Minnesota, with winning records. His 1986 season at Notre Dame was far from inspiring: five victories, six losses. However, most of the losses were against nationally ranked opponents. The Irish gave their fans a jolt of optimism at the end of the season with a 38–37 upset of Southern California—in California.

The next year provided an exciting indication of what was to come under Holtz's guidance. An 8-3 regular season led to a Cotton Bowl invitation. Although Notre Dame lost the bowl game to Texas A&M, fans sensed their team once again was on the brink of fame. Glory came the very next year when Notre Dame, undefeated, won the 1988 national championship. It was the university's eleventh football title.

Holtz coached Notre Dame through the 1996 season. He took the Irish to nine consecutive postseason bowl games, winning five.

On the practice field, Holtz was severely demanding. Some of his players called him "Lou-cifer," a devil-coach. Today, as a college football TV analyst, author, and motivational speaker,

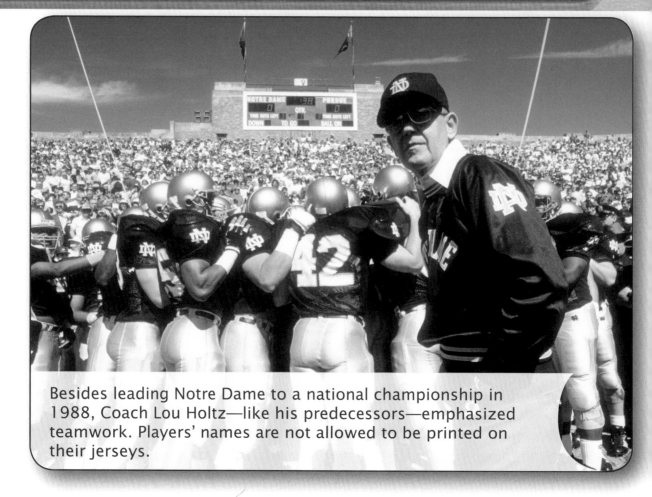

Besides leading Notre Dame to a national championship in 1988, Coach Lou Holtz—like his predecessors—emphasized teamwork. Players' names are not allowed to be printed on their jerseys.

Holtz projects an image of a comical, mild-mannered little grandfather—but extremely knowledgeable about football. *Sports Illustrated* writer Austin Murphy, in his book *Saturday Rules*, commented that Holtz "may have been the most charismatic coach of his generation."

Coaches Knute Rockne, Frank Leahy, Ara Parseghian, Dan Devine, and Lou Holtz were all elected to the College Football Hall of Fame.

CHAPTER 4

LEADERS ON THE FIELD

Great coaches naturally attract promising young players to their programs. The record books prove this has been true at the University of Notre Dame, especially under the coaching of Rockne, Leahy, Parseghian, and Holtz.

In all, Notre Dame has won eleven national championships and produced ninety-seven NCAA all-American players through the 2012 season. Unofficially, it can claim two additional national titles. (Not all of the rating organizations agreed on the top teams of 1938 and 1953.)

STAR PLAYERS

Seven Heisman Trophy winners played at Notre Dame—more than at any other university. They were quarterbacks Angelo Bertelli (1943), John Lujack (1947), and John Huarte (1964); halfback John Lattner (1953); halfback/kicker Paul Hornung (1956); tight end Leon Hart (1949); and wide receiver Tim Brown (1987).

Hundreds of players, although they did not win the coveted Heisman, will be long remembered by Notre Dame and professional football fans. The university's

Joe Theismann passes against Southern Cal in their 1968 tie. Theismann, who later played for the Washington Redskins, was one of many outstanding Notre Dame quarterbacks.

football yearbook lists some ten pages of all-time roster notables in fine print.

Notre Dame is especially known for its quarterbacks. Those who went on to National Football League (NFL) fame include Joe Theismann and Joe Montana. Theismann, who started from 1968 to 1970, set Notre Dame records for most passing yards and passing touchdowns in a season. He played for the Washington Redskins from 1974 to 1985.

Montana, considered one of the NFL's all-time best quarterbacks, started for Notre Dame late in his junior season (1977) and rose to stardom the next year. His most memorable college game was his last, the 1979 Cotton Bowl. Montana had the flu and missed much of the action while consuming warm chicken soup in the locker room. With Notre Dame trailing Houston, 34–12, late in the last quarter, Montana reentered the game and led the Irish to a 35–34 victory. The "Chicken Soup Game" is remembered fondly by all college football fans.

THE FOUR HORSEMEN

The famous "Four Horsemen of Notre Dame" pose in an amusing publicity photo in 1924. From left, the players are quarterback Harry Stuhldreher, fullback Elmer Layden, and halfbacks Jim Crowley and Don Miller.

The "Four Horsemen" of Notre Dame might not have been the greatest offensive backfield in college football history, but they remain the most famous.

In 1924, Coach Knute Rockne started Harry Stuhldreher at quarterback, Elmer Layden at fullback, and Don Miller and Jim Crowley at left and right halfback. (The "halfback" term is rarely used today. Offensive formations have become more complex. The modern "tailback" bears the responsibilities once performed by halfbackers.) Each player possessed exceptional talent. Sportswriters soon recognized that as a unit, they were the most effective offensive backfield in college football of their time. All were very fast, and they worked together with unusual cleverness. Remarkably, they all were quite small—just 158 pounds (71.7 kg) on average.

Much of the credit for their success rightfully belonged to their blockers. We rarely hear of them now, but the 1924 Notre Dame offensive linemen in their day were renowned as the "Seven Mules."

The 1924 team won all ten games, some of them against the best teams in America.

There have been many other latter-day greats on offense and defense. One of countless examples, Raghib "Rocket" Ismail (1989–1991), dazzled spectators nationwide as a receiver and kick returner. A teammate during those years was Chris Zorich, a punishing defensive tackle who was voted most valuable defensive player in the 1991 Orange Bowl.

THE GIPPER

No story of Notre Dame football would be complete without remembering George Gipp. In 1920, the powerful runner became the first Notre Dame player to make first team all-American. He is best remembered, though, for his tragic early death.

A Michigan native, Gipp enrolled at Notre Dame on a baseball scholarship. Coach Rockne discovered his natural football talents when he came across Gipp and another student drop-kicking a ball on the street.

Gipp was a wayward student. Although from a poor family, he always had money, winning bets at cards and billiards. Little interested in studies, he once was expelled for cutting too many classes. Gipp was allowed to play football anyway—mainly because the people of South Bend petitioned to keep him on the team. He usually skipped the first half of the week of practice, and when he attended, he was often late. But he was a star player at halfback, passer, kicker, and safety.

Gipp was Notre Dame's leading rusher and passer in 1918, 1919, and 1920. He was named to the all-American team at the end of the 1920 season, two weeks before his death from complications of pneumonia.

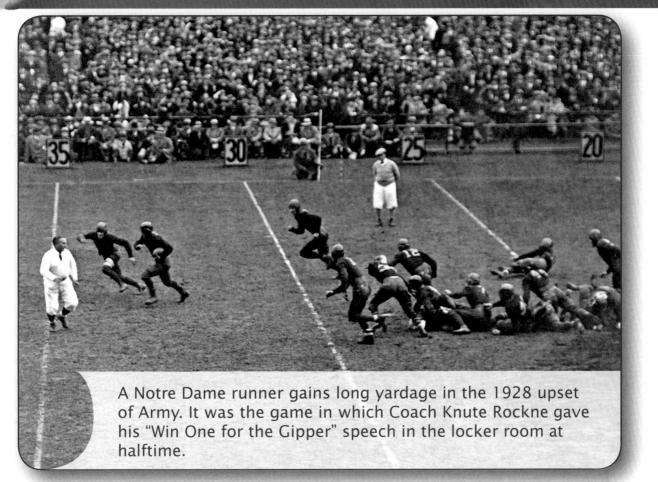

A Notre Dame runner gains long yardage in the 1928 upset of Army. It was the game in which Coach Knute Rockne gave his "Win One for the Gipper" speech in the locker room at halftime.

Coach Rockne later recounted a deathbed conversation he had with Gipp. "Some time, Rock," Gipp reportedly told him, "when the team is up against it, when things are wrong and the breaks are beating the boys, ask them to go in there with all they've got and win just one for the Gipper."

Eight years later, Rockne is said to have told the story to his team at halftime when they were losing to undefeated Army. The Irish, fired up in the second half, scored a 12–6 upset. "That's one for the Gipper," one of the Irish players stated.

"Win one for the Gipper" has become a rallying cry often uttered in seemingly hopeless circumstances.

NOT-SO-FAMOUS STANDOUTS

Not all of Notre Dame's heroes have been all-Americans or Heisman Trophy winners. One of the school's best-remembered victories was the 24–23 defeat of top-ranked Alabama in the 1973 Sugar Bowl. With two minutes to play, Notre Dame had the lead but faced a third down pinned at its own three-yard line. If forced to punt from its end zone, it would have given Alabama the ball around midfield, probably resulting in a game-winning Crimson Tide field goal.

Coach Ara Parseghian called a surprise pass play. Quarterback Tom Clements completed a thirty-six-yard pass to Robin Weber—a second-string tight end who had caught just one other pass during the regular season. The first down enabled Notre Dame to run out the clock and take the national championship.

A Notre Dame athlete who had a lifelong impact on his alma mater was Edward "Moose" Krause. As a football player (1931–1933), he was a star tackle who amazed teammates in a College All-Star Game by playing with a broken hand. Krause also excelled in basketball, baseball, and track and field.

During the 1940s and 1950s, Krause was head basketball coach and assistant football coach at Notre Dame. He was named athletics director in 1949 and served for thirty-two years. Krause died in 1992.

CHAPTER 5

NOTRE DAME IN THE NEW CENTURY

Excitement builds to fever pitch at many collegiate campuses as game day approaches on autumn Saturdays. At the University of Notre Dame, football fanfare and pride are virtually electric. Each week of every season brings renewed expectations.

Many Fighting Irish customs and celebrations, meanwhile, go back more than a century. Sportswriters for years have referred to the "Notre Dame mystique," an indefinable quality that seems to make the campus special. When asked to explain it, coach Lou Holtz once responded, "If you were there, no explanation is necessary. If you weren't, no explanation is satisfactory."

FIGHTING IRISH TRADITIONS

The Notre Dame football team today wears uniforms of navy blue and gold. Interestingly, green—the color associated with Ireland—has been the jersey color in the past. Ara Parseghian switched from green to blue while he was head coach. Dan Devine returned to green. Lou Holtz then changed back to blue.

Notre Dame jerseys were green during the Dan Devine coaching era. Notice the absence of markings on the gold helmets. The quarterback in this 1976 game was Joe Montana.

Unlike most college and professional football teams, Notre Dame players wear unmarked helmets. There are no numbers, colorful stripes, university initials, or touchdown stars. Student boosters repaint the gold helmets on Fridays before game days.

When Holtz became head coach in 1986, he insisted that players' names not be shown on their jerseys. He wanted to stress that they were playing as a team, not as individual standouts.

Notre Dame was the first university to field a marching band to support its football team. (Actually, the band was formed in 1846, long before football began at Notre Dame.) The school's "Victory March," first performed in 1909, has been called "the most stirring of all college pep songs."

The colorfully kilted Irish Guard, a ten-member precision unit, marches robotically into Notre Dame Stadium before the football team's explosive entry. They were made part of the marching band in 1949. Highly competitive tryouts are held for guard participation each year. (Among other traits, successful candidates must stand at least 6 feet 2 inches [1.9 m].)

CAMPUS LANDMARKS

Visitors to the campus are impressed by a number of landmarks. The Basilica of the Sacred Heart is a majestic Gothic cathedral noted particularly for its stained glass. The Grotto, constructed in 1896, is a scale model of a famous Catholic stone shrine in France. Some of its stones weigh more than 2 tons (1.8 metric tons). An array of lit candles highlight the scene at night, especially on football weekends.

Towering outside the stadium is a 138-foot (42-meter) mural of Jesus titled *Word of Life.* Composed of 374 granite panels, it is one of the most famous monuments on a university campus, easily recognized as a symbol of Notre Dame.

The massive Main Building, headquarters of the university administration, is striking for its gigantic golden dome. Notre Dame students are nicknamed "domers."

HISTORIC RIVALRIES AND UNFORGETTABLE GAMES

Notre Dame's longtime rivals include the Michigan Wolverines, Michigan State Spartans, USC Trojans, Purdue Boilermakers, and Navy Midshipmen. Austin Murphy, author of *Saturday Rules,* rated the annual Notre Dame–USC game the third-greatest rivalry in college football.

Dozens of past football games are considered classics by Notre Dame sports historians and fans. The 1913 victory over Army remains perhaps the most famous. The 1928 defeat of Army is remembered because of Knute Rockne's "Gipper" speech to his players at halftime. Others deemed especially significant include these.

* The 18–13 upset of Ohio State in 1935. The Ohio State Buckeyes had slaughtered their opponents all season long and were favored by as much as forty points. Many Notre Dame fans call it the "game of the century."

* The scoreless tie against Army in 1946. Notre Dame faithful consider it a victory because Army had a twenty-five-game winning streak and had trounced the Irish the two previous years, 59–0 and 48–0.

* The 7–0 victory over Oklahoma in 1957. It was another great upset because the Oklahoma Sooners, the defending national champion, were riding an incredible forty-seven-game winning streak spanning more than four years.

* The 24–11 Cotton Bowl win over Texas at the end of the 1970 season. It was especially sweet to "domers" because Texas had beaten Notre Dame in the previous Cotton Bowl.

* The 31–30 defeat of No. 1–ranked Miami in 1988.

* The 31–24 victory over Florida State in 1993. Also considered the "game of the century" by some, it is a fan favorite because the No. 2–ranked Irish beat the No. 1 Seminoles.

NOTRE DAME'S FOOTBALL PROGRAM TODAY

Notre Dame had mostly unimpressive seasons from the mid-1990s until 2012. The 2002 team provided a thrilling exception. Tyrone Willingham took charge as head coach that year, and the Fighting Irish opened the season with eight victories. In a cover article, *Sports Illustrated* magazine marveled at Notre Dame's "Return to Glory." The team then began to

The Alabama Crimson Tide (in white and red) spoiled Notre Dame's 2012 dream season, defeating the Fighting Irish in the BCS championship game. Here, quarterback Everett Golson scores a late, futile Irish touchdown.

struggle and ended the year with a record of 10–3. It was the university's best season in recent years—but 2003 was a disaster, and Willingham was fired at the end of 2004.

Sports forecasters had only modest expectations for Notre Dame as the 2012 season began. Brian Kelly was entering his third year as head coach with an unremarkable record of 14-10. However, after its opening victory against Navy in the game played in Ireland, the team returned home and continued to win. The Fighting Irish were unbeaten during the regular season but lost to Alabama in the BCS championship game.

In 2012, Notre Dame University announced it would join the Atlantic Coast Conference, a leading conference

CHAMPIONSHIP ACADEMICS

Apart from its athletic renown, Notre Dame University has been recognized for many years for setting high academic standards. Forbes.com ranked it twelfth among *America's Best Colleges* in 2012. To earn athletic scholarships at Notre Dame, football players must enter with excellent high school grade records—and keep them up.

In his book *Bowled Over: Big-Time College Football from the Sixties to the BCS Era*, author Michael Oriard ranks Notre Dame academically as "among the football superelite."

While scholastic dedication is emphasized, so is public service by the student body. More than 80 percent of Notre Dame students perform community service during their college years.

in major college sports. Only twenty-two of its twenty-six varsity sports teams are competing fully in the ACC, though. The most notable exception is the Fighting Irish football team, which has always been independent, belonging to no conference. Independence gives Notre Dame freedom to schedule games with a variety of opponents across the country.

As part of the ACC arrangement, Notre Dame has agreed to schedule five football games each season against ACC teams. This is forcing the athletics department to break off certain longstanding rivalries. To fans and observers, an especially disturbing decision was to end, after 2014, the historic series with the University of Michigan—Notre Dame's first football opponent in 1887.

A sea of students in green in Notre Dame Stadium in South Bend, Indiana. The school's long history of prominence has cultivated a "Notre Dame spirit" among supporters that is exceptional in college football.

A UNIVERSAL GLOW OF ENTHUSIASM

No matter who the opponents are, it's obvious the Fighting Irish can count on passionate support from their fans. Win or lose, the pageantry and emotional energy in South Bend on football Saturdays is unmatched.

Joe Theismann, who played quarterback for Notre Dame (1968–1970) and later for the Washington Redskins in the NFL, summarized campus excitement for the football program. "If you could find a way to bottle the Notre Dame spirit," he remarked, "you could light up the universe."

TIMELINE

1842: The founding of L'Université de Notre Dame du Lac.

1887: Notre Dame loses its first intercollegiate football game to the University of Michigan.

1896: Frank Hering, a player-coach, sets Notre Dame on a winning path in football.

1913: Notre Dame upsets Army in perhaps its most famous victory.

1918: Knute Rockne is named head football coach.

1929: Construction begins on Notre Dame Stadium.

1931: Knute Rockne is killed in an airplane crash.

1935: Notre Dame's famous upset of heavily favored Ohio State in the "game of the century."

1941: Frank Leahy becomes Notre Dame's head football coach.

1953: Coach Frank Leahy resigns with health problems.

1957: The Irish end Oklahoma's forty-seven-game winning streak.

1964: The glorious "Era of Ara" begins under head coach Ara Parseghian.

1971: Notre Dame beats Texas in the Cotton Bowl, redeeming its previous bowl loss.

1974: Dan Devine replaces Ara Parseghian as Notre Dame head football coach.

1986: Lou Holtz becomes head coach.

1988: Notre Dame wins its most recent national championship.

1996: Coach Lou Holtz resigns.

1997: Notre Dame Stadium is expanded to seat more than eighty thousand.

2002: The Fighting Irish under coach Tyrone Willingham achieve a 10–3 season record.

2012: Notre Dame University announces partial athletic affiliation with the Atlantic Coast Conference; its football team is undefeated during the regular season and unexpectedly earns No. 1 ranking; the Irish lose to Alabama in the BCS championship game.

GLOSSARY

academic Related to scholastic studies.

alma mater The school a person attended.

alumni People who attended or graduated from a particular school.

classical studies School courses in art, language, philosophy, science, etc., rather than mechanical trades.

gridiron Football field.

intercollegiate Related to competition (or cooperation) among two or more colleges and/or universities.

intramural Related to competition among teams or individuals attending the same school.

lacrosse Game in which players use sticks to maneuver a ball between goals.

logo Symbol designed to identify a school or product brand for publicity purposes.

moisture-wicking Related to a fabric engineered to control perspiration.

moleskin Heavy cloth, usually of cotton.

petition Collection of signatures by people requesting a certain action by a government or administrative authority.

rugby Historic game related to American football, but less regulated and more physically exhaustive.

scrimmage line The place on the football field where opposing teams face off to begin a play.

shamrock A three-leaved plant commonly associated with Ireland.

American Football Coaches Association (AFCA)

100 Legends Lane

Waco, TX 76706

(254) 754-7373

Web site: http://www.afca.com

The professional association of eleven thousand member coaches publishes weekly college football rankings and sponsors its own all-American player selections each year.

College Football Hall of Fame

111 South St. Joseph Street

South Bend, IN 46601

(800) 440-3263

Web site: http://www.collegefootball.org

Sponsored by the National Football Foundation, the Hall of Fame honors more than one thousand players and coaches who have participated in the sport since 1869.

Heisman Memorial Trophy

111 Broadway, Suite 103A

New York, NY 10006

(212) 425-7000

Web site: http://www.heisman.com

This organization awards the annual Heisman Trophy and publishes information on past winners.

National Collegiate Athletic Association (NCAA)

700 West Washington Street

P.O. Box 6222

Indianapolis, IN 46206-6222

(317) 917-6222

Web site: http://www.ncaa.org

This is the administrative headquarters of the NCAA.

University of Notre Dame

Notre Dame, IN 46556

(574) 631-5000

Web site: http://www.nd.edu

The Web site provides complete information about the university.

Walter Camp Football Foundation

P.O. Box 1663

New Haven, CT 06507

Web site: http://www.waltercamp.org

Named after Walter Camp, a pioneering organizer of college football, the foundation selects an all-America team each year.

WEB SITES

Due to the changing nature of Internet links, Rosen Publishing has developed an online list of Web sites related to the subject of this book. This site is updated regularly. Please use this link to access the list:

http://www.rosenlinks.com/AMWT/NDFB

FOR FURTHER READING

Aretha, David. *The Notre Dame Fighting Irish Football Team* (Great Sports Teams). Berkeley Heights, NJ: Enslow Publishers, 2001.

Callahan, Sean. *A Is for Ara: The ABCs of Notre Dame Football.* Chicago, IL: Eddy Street Press, 2007.

Frederick, Shane Gerald. *The Best of Everything Football Book* (Sports Illustrated Kids: The All-Time Best of Sports). North Mankato, MN: Capstone Press, 2011.

Green, David. *101 Reasons to Love Notre Dame Football.* New York, NY: Stewart, Tabori & Chang, 2009.

Jacobs, Greg. *The Everything KIDS' Football Book.* 3rd ed. Avon, MA: Adams Media, 2012.

Sports Illustrated for Kids. *Sports Illustrated Kids 1st and 10: Top 10 Lists of Everything in Football.* New York, NY: Sports Illustrated, 2011.

Sports Illustrated for Kids. *Sports Illustrated Kids Football Playbook: Games, Activities, Puzzles and Fun!* New York, NY: Sports Illustrated, 2011.

Wargin, Kathy-Jo. *Win One for the Gipper: America's Football Hero* (True Story). Ann Arbor, MI: Sleeping Bear Press, 2011.

Yuen, Kevin. *The 10 Most Intense College Football Rivalries.* New York, NY: Children's Press, 2008.

BIBLIOGRAPHY

Ara Parseghian Medical Research Foundation. "Coach Ara Parseghian Career Highlights." Retrieved November 2012 (http://www.parseghian.org).

Beard, Aaron. "Notre Dame to ACC in All Sports but Football." Associated Press, September 12, 2012. Retrieved September 2012 (http://sports.yahoo.com/news).

Boyles, Bob, and Paul Guido. *The USA Today College Football Encyclopedia.* New York, NY: Skyhorse Publishing, 2011.

Brondfield, Jerry. *Rockne: The Coach, the Man, the Legend.* Lincoln, NE: University of Nebraska Press, 2009.

Dent, Jim. *Resurrection: The Miracle Season That Saved Notre Dame.* New York, NY: Thomas Dunne Books/ St. Martin's Press, 2009.

LaFleur, Pete. "Magical 1964 Season Marked Debut of the Era of Ara." Notre Dame Fighting Irish Athletics Web site. Retrieved November 2012 (www.und.com/sports/m-footbl/spec-rel/ 100804aak.html).

Murphy, Austin. *Saturday Rules.* New York, NY: HarperCollins Publishers, 2007.

Oriard, Michael. *Bowled Over: Big-Time College Football from the Sixties to the BCS Era.* Chapel Hill, NC: The University of North Carolina Press, 2009.

Pont, Sally. *Fields of Honor: The Golden Age of College Football and the Men Who Created It.* New York, NY: Harcourt, 2001.

INDEX

ABOUT THE AUTHOR

Daniel E. Harmon is an author of more than eighty books and thousands of magazine and newspaper articles. His previous sports books include *Grappling and Submission Grappling* (Mixed Martial Arts). A former sports writer and editor, he once almost died chasing an opposing back while researching an article on rugby.

PHOTO CREDITS

Cover, p. 1 Ezra Shaw/Getty Images; back cover (goal post) David Lee/Shutterstock.com; pp. 4, 10 Collegiate Images /Getty Images; p. 5 Barry Cronin/Getty Images; pp. 7, 13, 20, 27, 33 © iStockphoto.com/John Rodriguez; p. 8 North Wind Picture Archives/AP Images; pp. 12, 31 Underwood Archives/Archive Photos/Getty Images; pp. 15, 18, 21, 23 © AP Images; pp. 26, 39 Jonathan Daniel/Getty Images; p. 28 James Flores/ WireImage/Getty Images; p. 29 Notre Dame University/Getty Images; p. 34 Focus on Sport/Getty Images; p. 37 Streeter Lecka/Getty Images; multiple interior page borders and boxed text backgrounds (football) Nickola_Che /Shutterstock.com; back cover and multiple interior pages background (abstract pattern) © iStockphoto.com/Che McPherson.

Designer: Brian Garvey; Editor: Kathy Kuhtz Campbell; Photo Researcher: Marty Levick